PIANO • VOCAL • GUITAR

2nd EDITION

ULTIMATE

CHILDREN'S Songbook

ISBN 978-0-6343-02181-7

HAL•LEONARD®
CORPORATION

7777 W. BLUEMOUND RD. P.O. BOX 13819 MILWAUKEE, WI 53213

Visit Hal Leonard Online at
www.halleonard.com

PIANO · VOCAL · GUITAR
ULTIMATE
CHILDREN'S Songbook

THE ADDAMS FAMILY THEME
Theme from the TV Show and Movie

Music and Lyrics by
VIC MIZZY

ALLEY CAT SONG

Words by JACK HARLEN
Music by FRANK BJORN

He goes on the prowl each night like an al-ley cat,

look-in' for some new de-light like an al-ley cat.

She can't trust him out of sight, there's no doubt of that.
He don't know what "faith-ful" means, there's no doubt of that.

ALPHABET SONG

Traditional

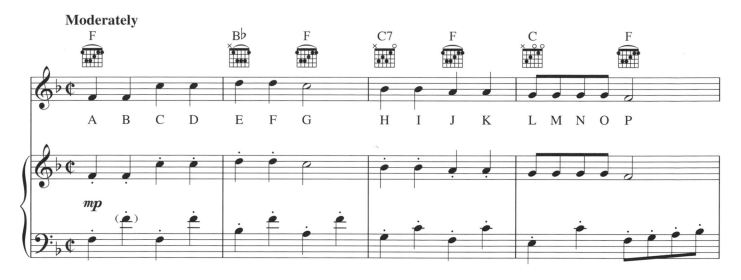

A B C D E F G H I J K L M N O P

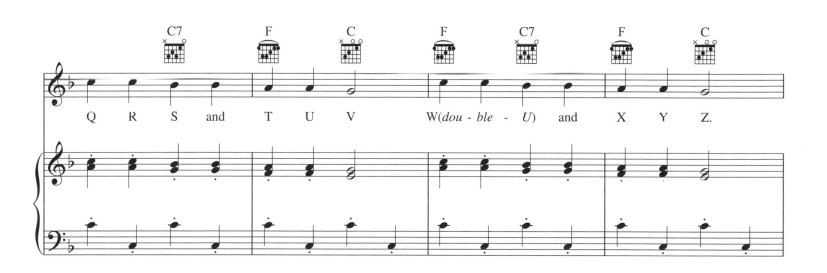

Q R S and T U V W(dou - ble - U) and X Y Z.

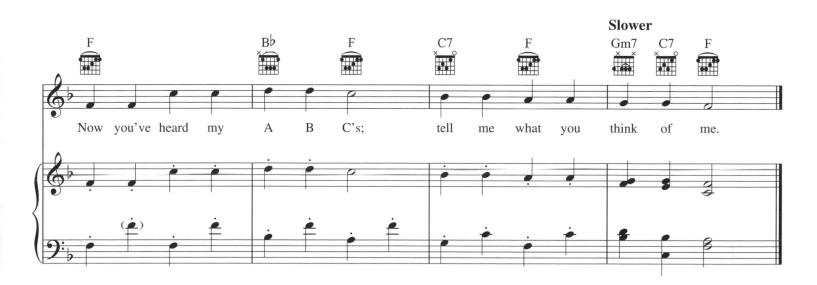

Now you've heard my A B C's; tell me what you think of me.

ANIMAL FAIR

American Folk Song

ANY DREAM WILL DO
from JOSEPH AND THE AMAZING TECHNICOLOR® DREAMCOAT

Music by ANDREW LLOYD WEBBER
Lyrics by TIM RICE

JOSEPH:
I closed my eyes drew back the cur - tain to see for cer - tain what I thought I knew. Far far a-

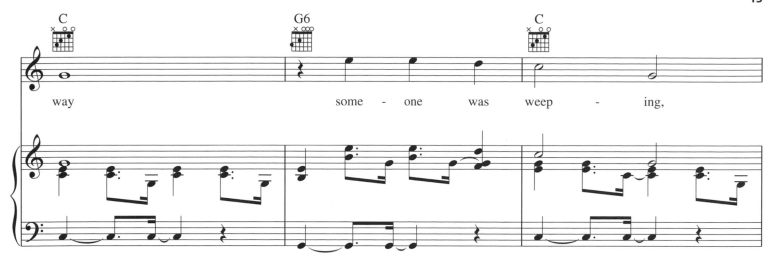

way   some - one was weep - ing,

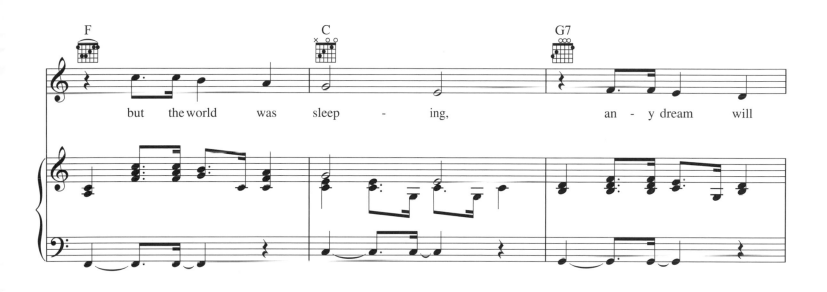

but the world was sleep - ing,   an - y dream will

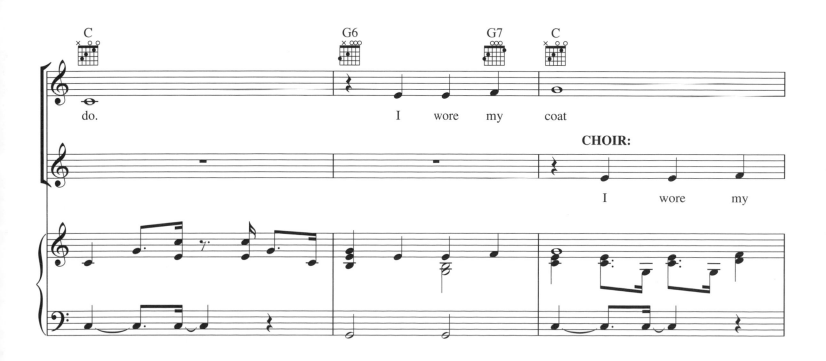

do.   I wore my coat

CHOIR:

I wore my

BE KIND TO YOUR WEB-FOOTED FRIENDS

Traditional

THE BARE NECESSITIES

from Walt Disney's THE JUNGLE BOOK

Words and Music by
TERRY GILKYSON

To Coda ⊕

fond - er _____ of my big home.
raw paw, _____ well, next time, be - ware.

Baloo: The bees are buzz - ing in the tree _____ to make some

hon - ey, just _____ for me. When you look un - der the

rocks and plants, _____ take a glance at the fan - cy ants _____ and

24

BIBBIDI-BOBBIDI-BOO

(The Magic Song)

from Walt Disney's CINDERELLA

Words by JERRY LIVINGSTON
Music by MACK DAVID and AL HOFFMAN

Brightly

Sa-la-ga-doo-la men-chic-ka boo-la

bib-bi-di-bob-bi-di-boo. Put 'em to-geth-er and what have you got bib-bi-di-bob-bi-di-boo.

Sa-la-ga-doo-la men-chic-ka boo-la bib-bi-di-bob-bi-di-boo. It-'ll do mag-ic be-lieve it or not,

BINGO

Traditional

NOTE: Each time a letter of BINGO is deleted in the lyric,
clap your hands in place of singing the letter.

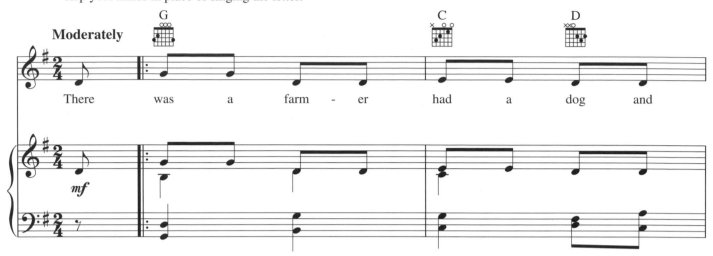

There was a farm - er had a dog and

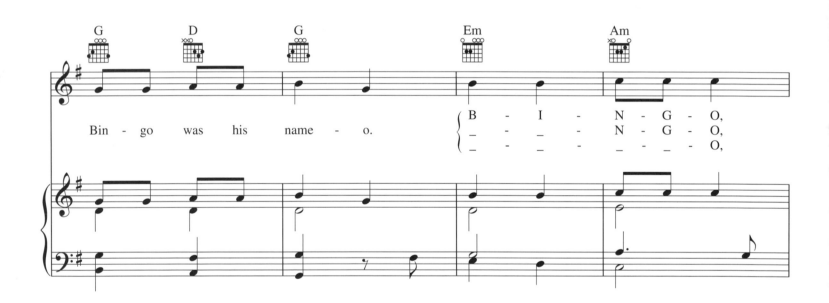

Bin - go was his name - o.

{ B - I - N - G - O,
  _ - _ - _ - N - G - O,
  _ - _ - _ - _ - _ - O,

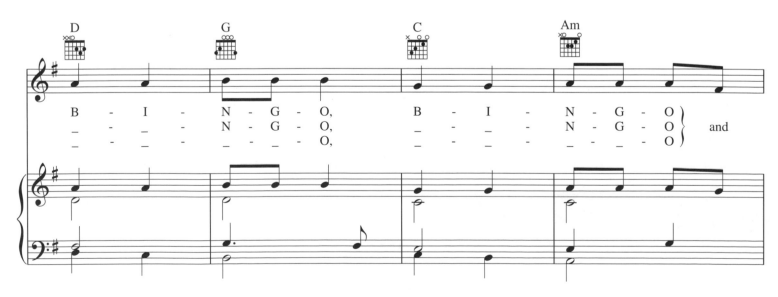

B - I - N - G - O,   B - I - N - G - O }
_ - _ - _ - N - G - O,   _ - _ - _ - N - G - O   and
_ - _ - _ - _ - O,   _ - _ - _ - _ - _ - O)

29

THE BRADY BUNCH
Theme from the Paramount Television Series THE BRADY BUNCH

Words and Music by SHERWOOD SCHWARTZ
and FRANK DEVOL

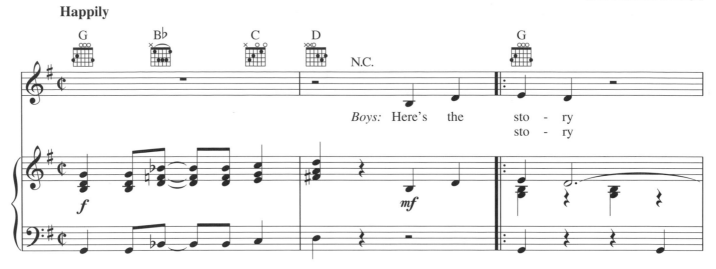

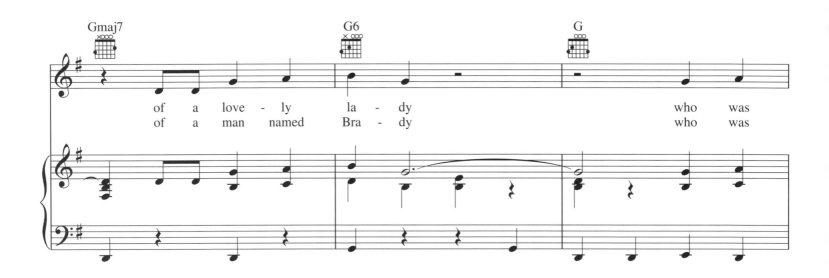

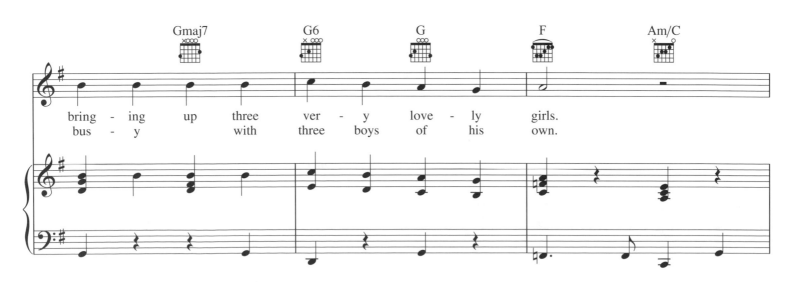

THE CANDY MAN

from WILLY WONKA AND THE CHOCOLATE FACTORY

Words and Music by LESLIE BRICUSSE
and ANTHONY NEWLEY

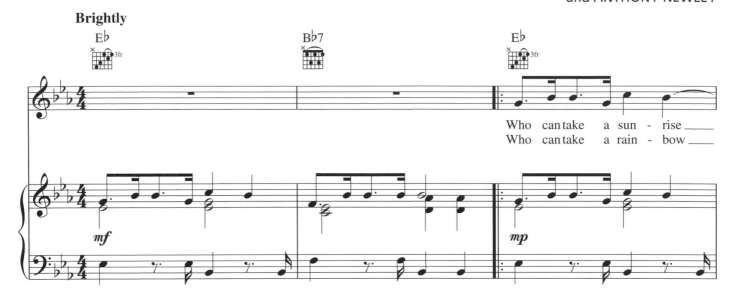

THE CHICKEN DANCE

By TERRY RENDALL
and WERNER THOMAS

1. Do you wan-na feel good,
2.-4. *(See additional lyrics)*

wan-na laugh and play? (Let's laugh and play.) Wan-na have some fun,

throw your blues a - way? (Your blues a - way.) Are you feel-in' sad?

Additional Lyrics

2. Hey, you're in the swing.
You're cluckin' like a bird. (Pluck, pluck, pluck, pluck.)
You're flappin' your wings.
Don't you feel absurd. (No, no, no, no.)
It's a chicken dance,
Like a rooster and a hen. (Ya, ya, ya, ya.)
Flappy chicken dance;
Let's do it again. *(To Chorus 2:)*

Chorus 2:
Relax and let the music move you.
Let all your inhibitions go.
Just watch your partner whirl around you.
We're havin' fun now; I told you so.

3. Now you're flappin' like a bird
And you're wigglin' too. (I like that move.)
You're without a care.
It's a dance for you. (Just made for you.)
Keep doin' what you do.
Don't you cop out now. (Don't cop out now.)
Gets better as you dance;
Catch your breath somehow.
Chorus

4. Now we're almost through,
Really flyin' high. (Bye, bye, bye, bye.)
All you chickens and birds,
Time to say goodbye. (To say goodbye.)
Goin' back to the nest,
But the flyin' was fun. (Oh, it was fun.)
Chicken dance was the best,
But the dance is done.

EENSY WEENSY SPIDER

Traditional

DO-RE-MI
from THE SOUND OF MUSIC

Lyrics by OSCAR HAMMERSTEIN II
Music by RICHARD RODGERS

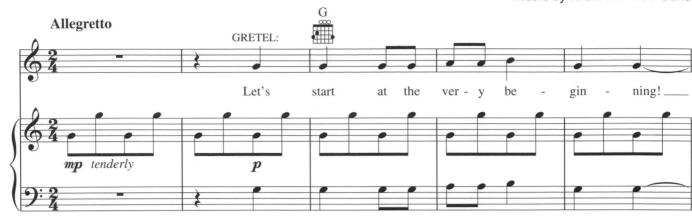

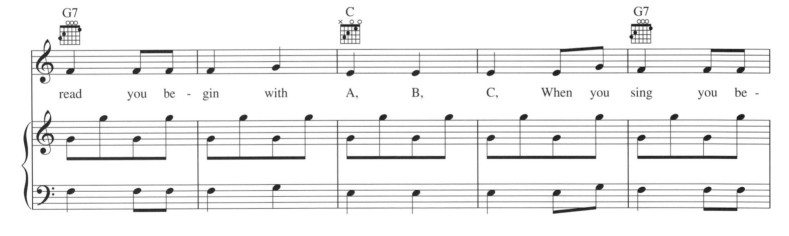

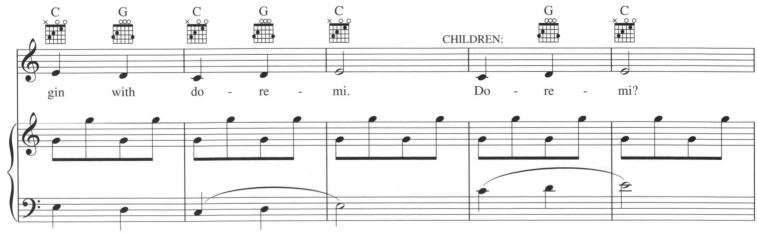

DO YOUR EARS HANG LOW?

Traditional

Do your (D.S.) ears hang low? Do they
Can your ears hang stand low? high? Can they

THE GROUCH SONG
from the Television Series SESAME STREET

Words and Music by
JEFF MOSS

Moderately, with a beat

(Spoken:) *Grizzy: So Elmo, what do you think it takes to be a grouch?*   *Elmo: Well, Elmo could sing about it, Grizzy.*
Grizzy: I can't wait to

Elmo: If you wake up in the morn - ing mean and grump-y,   and you
hear this. Oscar: This could be a mistake.

frown at ev-'ry-bod - y that you see,   *Grizzy:* and if you like your oat-meal nice and cold and

THE FARMER IN THE DELL

Traditional

Additional Lyrics

3. The wife takes a child, etc.

4. The child takes a nurse, etc.

5. The nurse takes a dog, etc.

6. The dog takes a cat, etc.

7. The cat takes a rat, etc.

8. The rat takes the cheese, etc.

9. The cheese stands alone, etc.

FRIEND LIKE ME

from Walt Disney's ALADDIN

Words by HOWARD ASHMAN
Music by ALAN MENKEN

GOIN' TO THE ZOO

Words and Music by
TOM PAXTON

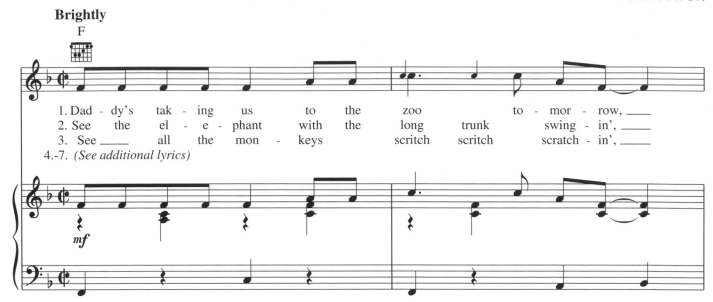

1. Dad-dy's tak-ing us to the zoo to-mor-row,
2. See the el-e-phant with the long trunk swing-in',
3. See all the mon-keys scritch scritch scratch-in',
4.-7. *(See additional lyrics)*

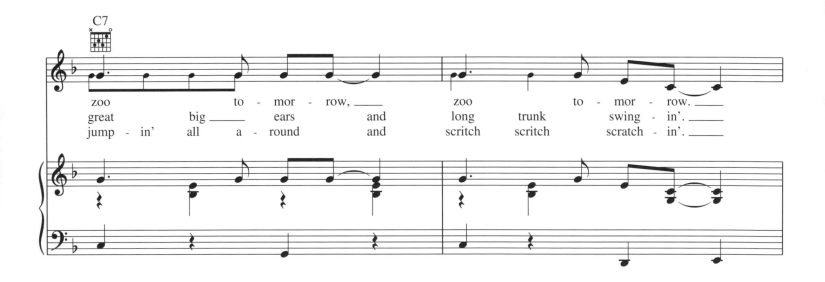

zoo to-mor-row, zoo to-mor-row.
great big ears and long trunk swing-in'.
jump-in' all a-round and scritch scritch scratch-in'.

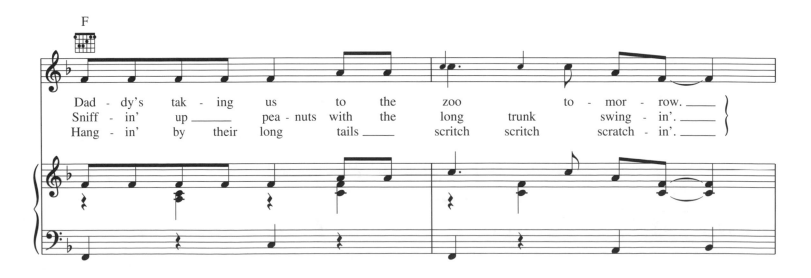

Dad-dy's tak-ing us to the zoo to-mor-row.
Sniff-in' up pea-nuts with the long trunk swing-in'.
Hang-in' by their long tails scritch scritch scratch-in'.

Additional Lyrics

4. Big black bear all huff huff a-puffin';
   Coat's too heavy, he's huff huff a-puffin'.
   Don't get too near the huff huff a-puffin',
   Or you won't stay all day.
   Chorus 1

5. Seals in the pool all honk honk honkin',
   Catchin' fish and honk honk honkin',
   Little seals honk honk honkin'.
   We can stay all day.
   Chorus 1

(slower tempo)

6. We stayed all day and we're gettin' sleepy,
   Sittin' in the car gettin' sleep sleep sleepy.
   Home already and we're sleep sleep sleepy.
   We have stayed all day.

   Chorus 2: We've been to the zoo, zoo, zoo.
   So have you, you, you.
   You came too, too, too.
   We've been to the zoo, zoo, zoo.

(original tempo)

7. Momma's taking us to the zoo tomorrow,
   Zoo tomorrow, zoo tomorrow.
   Momma's taking us to the zoo tomorrow;
   We can stay all day.
   Chorus 1

HAKUNA MATATA
from Walt Disney Pictures' THE LION KING

Music by ELTON JOHN
Lyrics by TIM RICE

HAPPY TRAILS
from the Television Series THE ROY ROGERS SHOW

Words and Music by
DALE EVANS

HELLO MUDDUH, HELLO FADDUH!

(A Letter from Camp)

Words and Music by ALLAN SHERMAN
and LOU BUSCH

Medium tempo

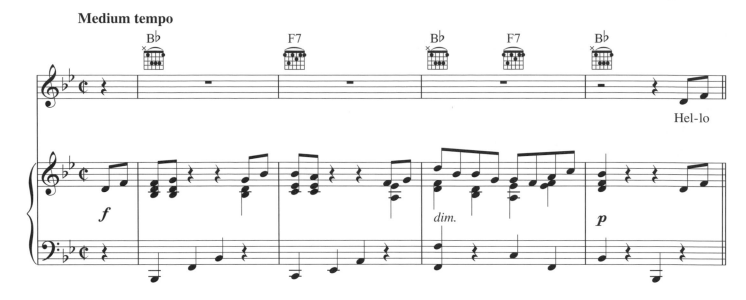

Hel-lo

Mud- duh,   hel - lo   Fad - duh,   here   I   am   at   Camp Gra-
coun-s'lors   hate the   wait - ers,   and   the   lake   has   al - li -

na - da;   Camp   is   ver - y   en - ter - tain - ing,   and they
ga - tors;   And the head-coach   wants   no   sis - sies,   so   he

I'M POPEYE THE SAILOR MAN

Theme from the Paramount Cartoon POPEYE THE SAILOR

Words and Music by
SAMMY LERNER

86

HUSH, LITTLE BABY

Carolina Folk Lullaby

IF YOU'RE HAPPY AND YOU KNOW IT

Words and Music by
L. SMITH

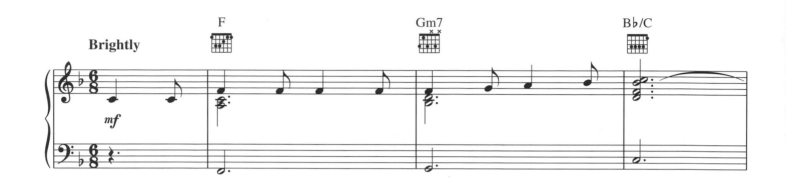

If you're hap - py and you know it, clap your
hap - py and you know it, tap your
hap - py and you know it, nod your

hands.   (clap,   clap)   If you're hap - py and you
toe.   (tap,   tap)   If you're hap - py and you
head.   (nod,   nod)   If you're hap - py and you

IN MY OWN LITTLE CORNER

from CINDERELLA

Lyrics by OSCAR HAMMERSTEIN II
Music by RICHARD RODGERS

Refrain (*with tender expression*)

cool and con-fi-dent kind of air, _____ Just as long as I stay in my own lit-tle cor-ner, _____ All a-lone in my own lit-tle chair. In my chair. _____

IT'S A SMALL WORLD

from "it's a small world" at Disneyland Park and Magic Kingdom Park

Words and Music by RICHARD M. SHERMAN
and ROBERT B. SHERMAN

THE MARVELOUS TOY

Words and Music by
TOM PAXTON

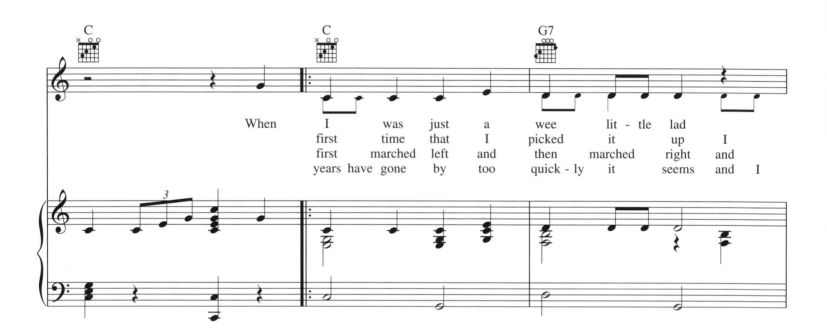

came one night, and gave to me a toy.
two big but-tons that looked like big green eyes.
it had gone, it was-n't e-ven there!
gave to him my mar-v'lous lit-tle toy.

A I

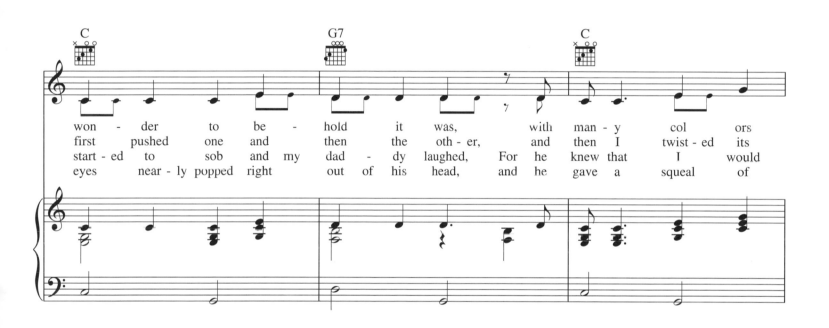

won - der to be - hold it was, with man - y col ors
first pushed one and then the oth - er, and then I twist - ed its
start - ed to sob and my dad - dy laughed, For he knew that I would
eyes near - ly popped right out of his head, and he gave a squeal of

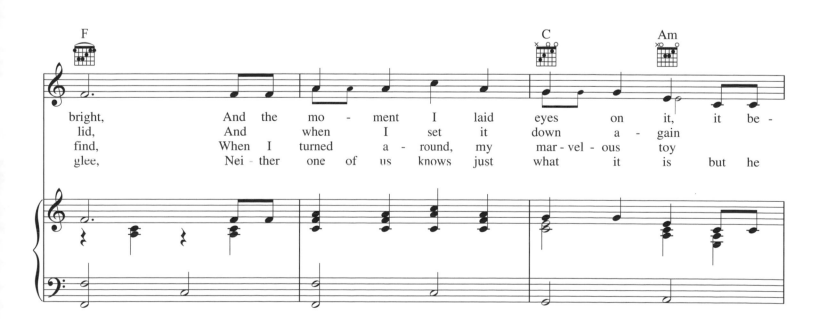

bright, And the mo - ment I laid eyes on it, it be-
lid, And when I set it down a - gain
find, When I turned a - round, my mar - vel - ous toy
glee, Nei - ther one of us knows just what it is but he

KUM BA YAH

Traditional Spiritual

LITTLE APRIL SHOWER

from Walt Disney's BAMBI

Words by LARRY MOREY
Music by FRANK CHURCHILL

Brightly and lightly

I nev-er mind how much it rains in A-pril.

I nev-er lose my tem-per and com-plain. If

you come down my way on an-y rain-y day, you'll

LITTLE WHITE DUCK

Lyrics by WALT WHIPPO
Music by BERNARD ZARITSKY

| | D7 | | | G | | | D7 |

said, "I'm glad I'm a lit - tle white duck sit - ting in the wa - ter."
said, "I'm glad I'm a lit - tle green frog swim-ming in the wa - ter."
said, "I'm glad I'm a lit - tle black bug float - ing on the wa - ter."

1-4 | G | D7 | 5 | G | D7 | G

Quack, quack, quack. (2.) There's a hoo.
Glumph, glumph, glumph. (3.) There's a
Chirp, chirp, chirp. (4.) There's a

Additional Lyrics

4. There's a little red snake
   Lying in the water,
   A little red snake
   Doing what he oughter.
   He frightened the duck and the frog so bad;
   He ate the little bug and he said,
   "I'm glad I'm a little red snake
   Lying in the water."
   Sss, sss, sss.

5. Now there's nobody left
   Sitting in the water,
   Nobody left
   Doing what he oughter.
   There's nothing left but the lily pad;
   The duck and the frog ran away.
   It's sad that there's nobody left
   Sitting in the water.
   Boo, hoo, hoo.

MAH-NÁ MAH-NÁ

By PIERO UMILIANI

Doo doo doo doo doo doo doo doo doo doo

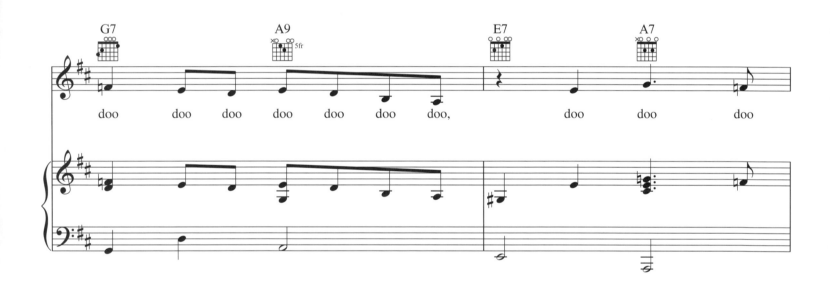

doo doo doo doo doo doo doo, doo doo doo

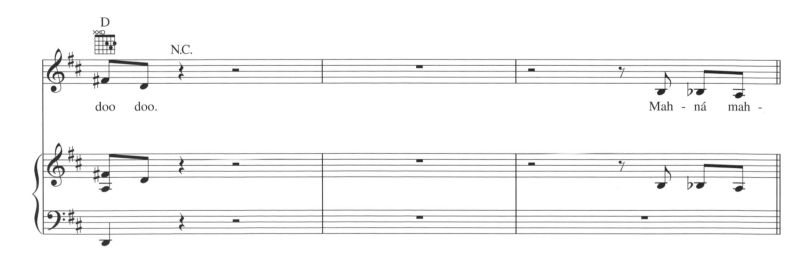

doo doo. Mah - ná mah -

MICKEY MOUSE MARCH

from Walt Disney's THE MICKEY MOUSE CLUB

Words and Music by
JIMMIE DODD

THE MUPPET SHOW THEME
from the Television Series

Words and Music by JIM HENSON
and SAM POTTLE

It's time to play the mu - sic. It's time to light the lights. _

It's time to meet the Mup - pets on *The Mup - pet Show* _ to-night.

THE NAME GAME

By LINCOLN CHASE
and SHIRLEY ELLISTON

fee fi mo-mar-mold. Ar-nold!

But if the first two let-ters are ev-er the same,

drop them both, then say the name. Like Bob, Bob, drop the

"B's." Bo - ob, or Fred. Fred, drop the "F's." Fo - red, or

OLD MACDONALD

Traditional Children's Song

1. Old Mac - Don - ald had a farm, E - I - E - I -
2. Old Mac - Don - ald had a farm, E - I - E - I -
3. Old Mac - Don - ald had a farm, E - I - E - I -
4.–6. *(See additional lyrics)*

O. _____ And on his farm he had a cow, E - I - E - I -
O. _____ And on his farm he had a pig, E - I - E - I -
O. _____ And on his farm he had a duck, E - I - E - I -

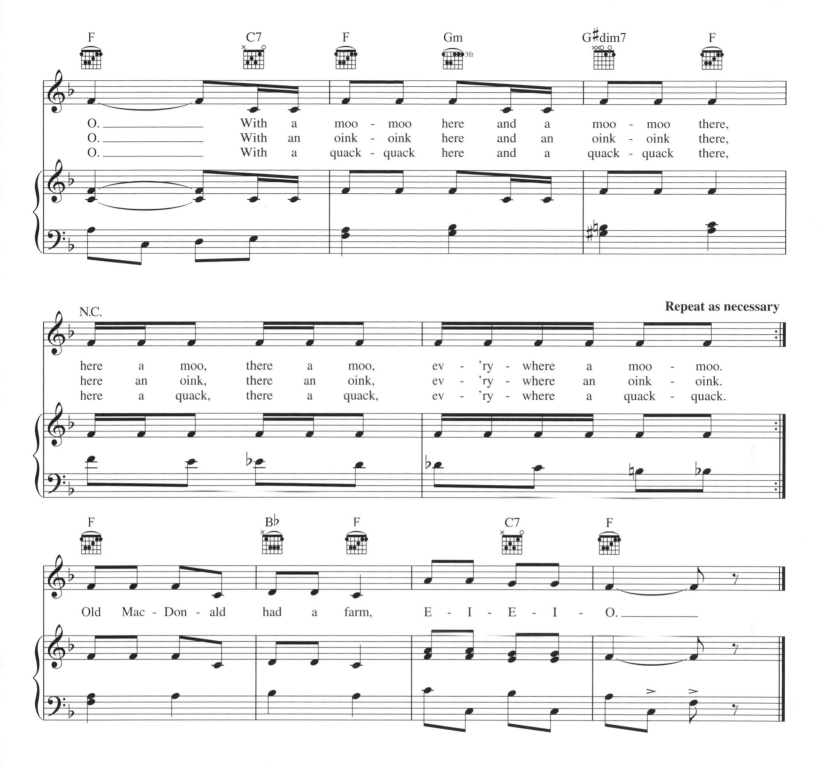

Additional Lyrics

4. Old MacDonald had a farm,
E-I-E-I-O,
And on his farm he had a horse,
E-I-E-I-O,
With a neigh-neigh here and a neigh-neigh there, etc.

5. Old MacDonald had a farm,
E-I-E-I-O,
And on his farm he had a donkey,
E-I-E-I-O,
With a hee-haw here and a hee-haw there, etc.

6. Old MacDonald had a farm,
E-I-E-I-O,
And on his farm he had some chickens,
E-I-E-I-O,
With a chick-chick here and a chick-chick there, etc.

ON TOP OF SPAGHETTI

Words and Music by
TOM GLAZER

ONE SMALL VOICE

from the Television Series SESAME STREET

Words and Music by
JEFF MOSS

PEANUT SAT ON A RAILROAD TRACK

Traditional

PEASE PORRIDGE HOT

Traditional

PETER, PETER, PUMPKIN EATER

Traditional

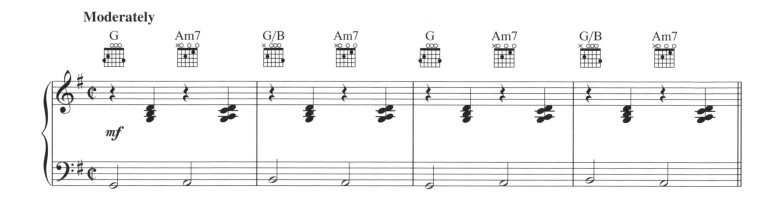

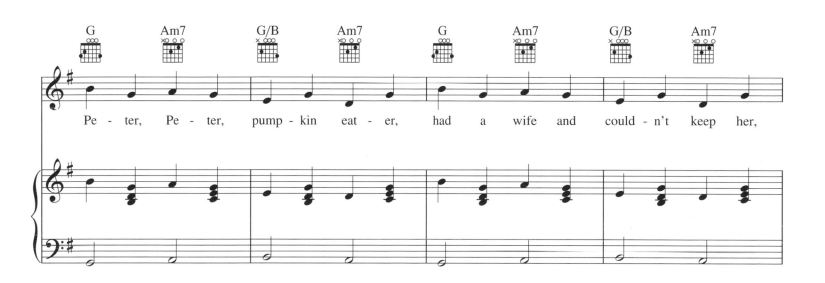

Pe - ter, Pe - ter, pump-kin eat - er, had a wife and could - n't keep her,

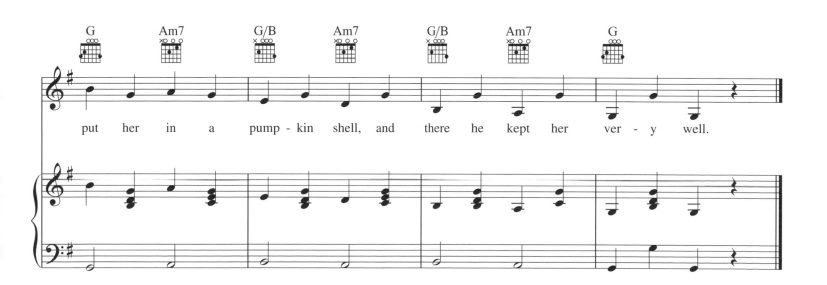

put her in a pump-kin shell, and there he kept her ver - y well.

THE RAINBOW CONNECTION
from THE MUPPET MOVIE

Words and Music by PAUL WILLIAMS
and KENNETH L. ASCHER

Why are there so man- y songs a- bout rain- bows, and
Who said that ev- 'ry wish would be heard and an- swered when

what's on the oth- er side? ____
wished on the morn- ing star? ____

Rain- bows are vi- sions, ___ but on- ly il- lu- sions, and
Some- bod- y thought of that, and some- one be- lieved it;

138

REFLECTION
from Walt Disney Pictures' MULAN

Music by MATTHEW WILDER
Lyrics by DAVID ZIPPEL

SESAME STREET THEME
from the Television Series SESAME STREET

Words by BRUCE HART,
JON STONE and JOE RAPOSO
Music by JOE RAPOSO

ROCK-A-BYE, BABY

Traditional

ROCKY & BULLWINKLE
from the Cartoon Television Series

By FRANK COMSTOCK

ROW, ROW, ROW YOUR BOAT

Traditional

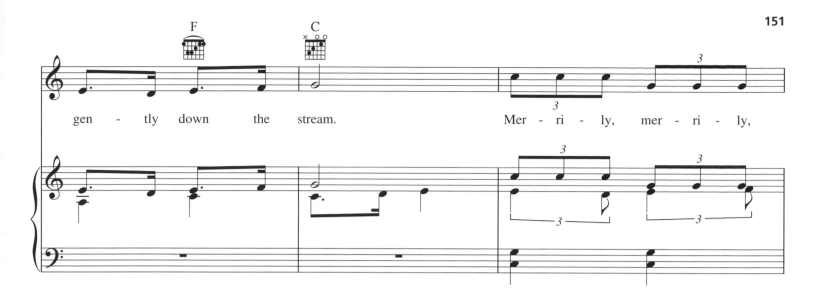

gen - tly down the stream. Mer - ri - ly, mer - ri - ly,

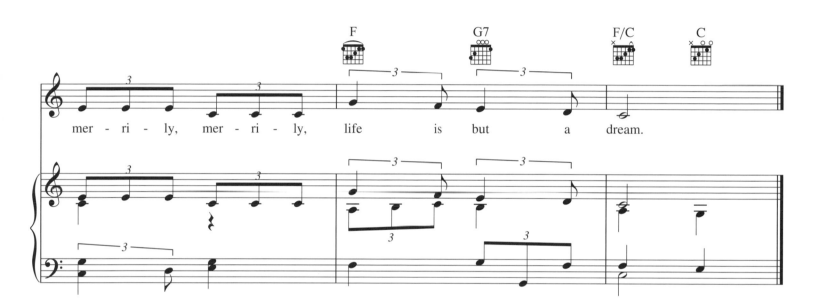

mer - ri - ly, mer - ri - ly, life is but a dream.

A SUGGESTED ACTIVITY

"Row, Row, Row Your Boat" is a famous "round" that has been sung and enjoyed
by people of all ages. When sung correctly, the melody actually goes around and
around. Here's how it works: The singers are divided into two groups.
The first group sings the first line alone. At this point, the second group starts at
the beginning, while the first group continues with the second line. In this manner,
the groups are always exactly one line apart as the tune is repeated.
The last time through, the second group sings the final line alone just as the first group
sang the opening line alone. Try it. . . it's fun!

RUBBER DUCKIE
from the Television Series SESAME STREET

Words and Music by
JEFF MOSS

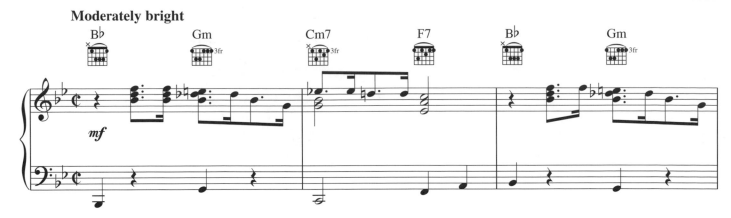

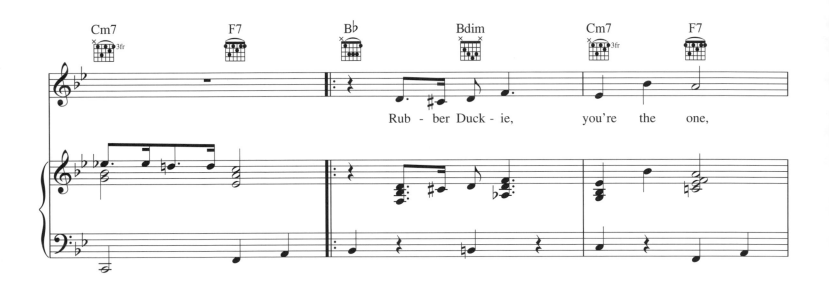

Rub - ber Duck - ie, you're the one,

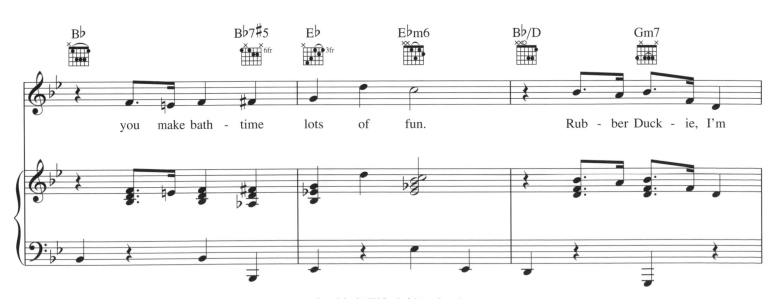

you make bath - time lots of fun. Rub - ber Duck - ie, I'm

RUMBLY IN MY TUMBLY

from Walt Disney's THE MANY ADVENTURES OF WINNIE THE POOH

Words and Music by RICHARD M. SHERMAN
and ROBERT B. SHERMAN

Easy Latin tempo

Hum-dum dum dum hum-dee dum dum,
I don't need a pot of hon-ey.

I'm so rum-bly in my tum-bly. Time to munch an ear-ly lunch-eon,
I'd be grate-ful for a plate-full. When I'm rum-bly in my tum-bly,

time for some-thing sweet! Oh, I would-n't climb this tree if a
then it's time to eat! It's the taste-ful thing to do, be it

THE SIAMESE CAT SONG
from Walt Disney's LADY AND THE TRAMP

Words and Music by PEGGY LEE
and SONNY BURKE

SO LONG, FAREWELL

from THE SOUND OF MUSIC

Lyrics by OSCAR HAMMERSTEIN II
Music by RICHARD RODGERS

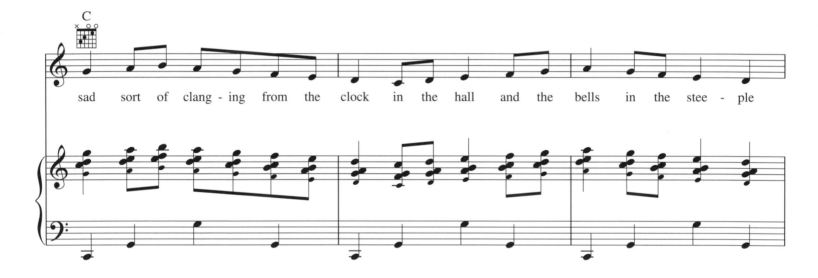

hate to go and miss this pret-ty sight. _

So long, fare-well, Auf wie-der-sehn, a-dieu, _ a-

CHILDREN:

KURT:

dieu, A-dieu, to yieu and yieu and yieu. _

So long, fare-well, Au' - voir, Auf wie-der - sehn, __ I'd

like to stay and taste my first cham - pagne. __

A SPOONFUL OF SUGAR

from Walt Disney's MARY POPPINS

Words and Music by RICHARD M. SHERMAN
and ROBERT B. SHERMAN

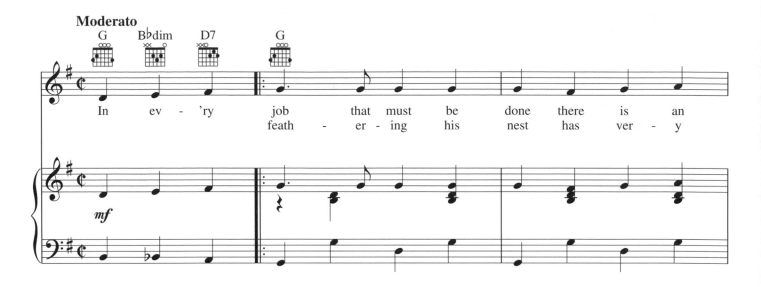

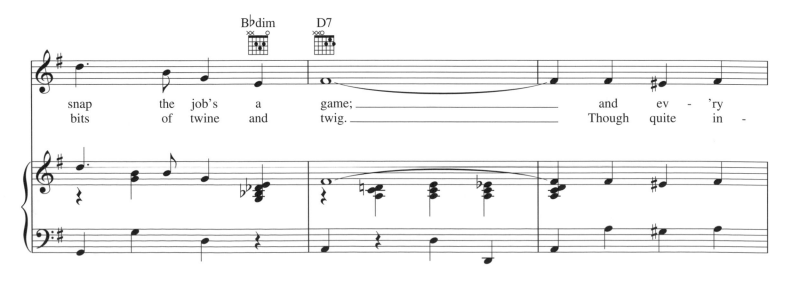

SUPERCALIFRAGILISTICEXPIALIDOCIOUS
from Walt Disney's MARY POPPINS

Words and Music by RICHARD M. SHERMAN
and ROBERT B. SHERMAN

Mary Poppins:
Su - per - cal - i - frag - il - is - tic - ex - pi - al - i - do - cious! E - ven though the sound of it is some - thing quite a - tro - cious, if you say it

TAKE ME OUT TO THE BALL GAME

Words by JACK NORWORTH
Music by ALBERT VON TILZER

Take me out to the ball game, take me out to the crowd. _____

WINNIE THE POOH

from Walt Disney's THE MANY ADVENTURES OF WINNIE THE POOH

Words and Music by RICHARD M. SHERMAN
and ROBERT B. SHERMAN

178

THIS LAND IS YOUR LAND

Words and Music by
WOODY GUTHRIE

Bright and cheerful

As I went

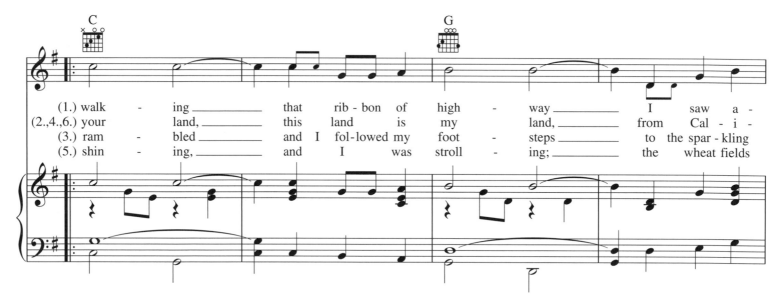

(1.) walk - ing _____ that rib - bon of high - way _____ I saw a -
(2.,4.,6.) your land, _____ this land is my land, _____ from Cal - i -
(3.) ram - bled _____ and I fol-lowed my foot - steps _____ to the spar - kling
(5.) shin - ing, _____ and I was stroll - ing; _____ the wheat fields

bove me _____ that end - less sky - way; _____ I saw be -
for - nia _____ to the New York is - land; _____ from the red - wood
sands of _____ her dia - mond des - erts; _____ while all a -
wav - ing _____ and the dust clouds roll - ing. _____ The fog was

THREE BLIND MICE

Traditional

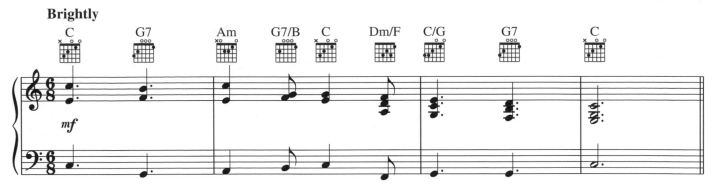

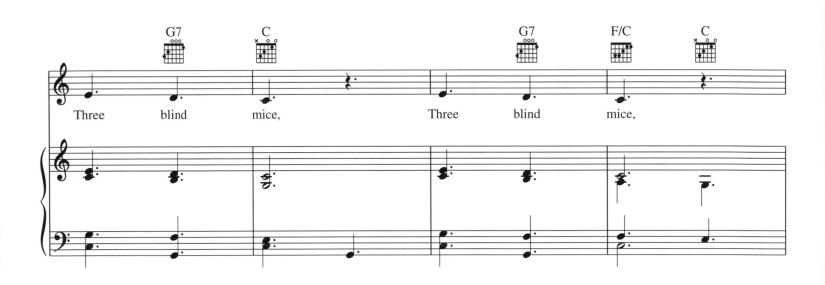

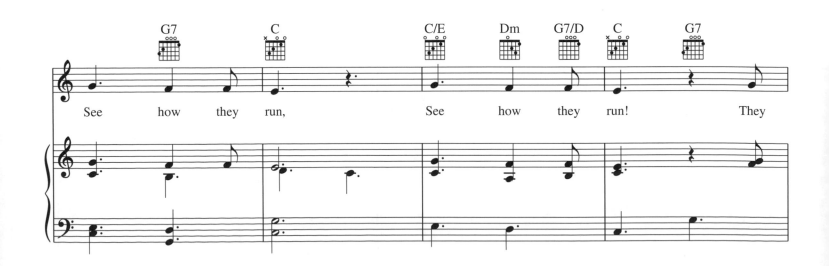

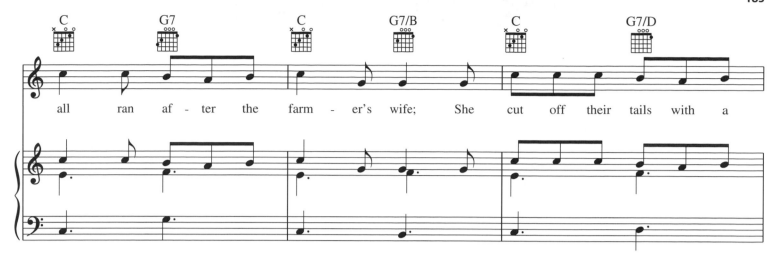

all ran af - ter the farm - er's wife; She cut off their tails with a

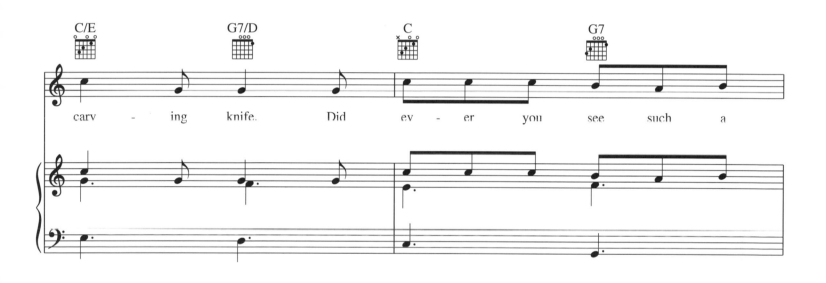

carv - ing knife. Did ev - er you see such a

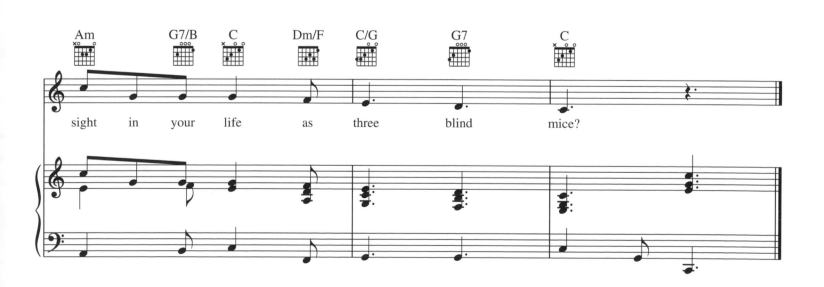

sight in your life as three blind mice?

THREE LITTLE FISHIES
(Itty Bitty Poo)

Words and Music by
SAXIE DOWELL

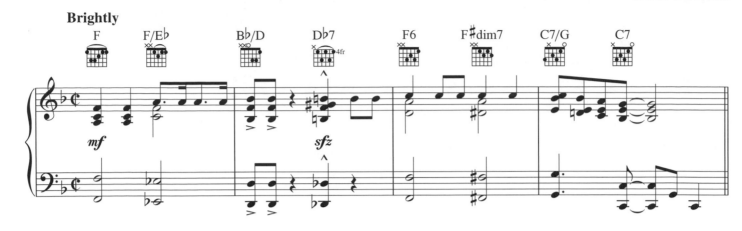

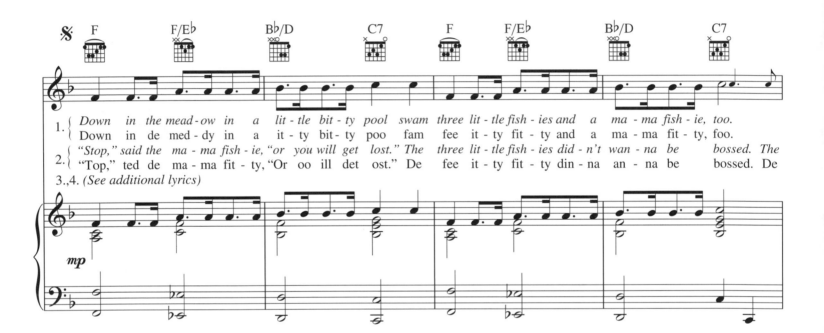

1. Down in the mead-ow in a lit-tle bit-ty pool swam three lit-tle fish-ies and a ma-ma fish-ie, too.
   Down in de med-dy in a it-ty bit-ty poo fam fee it-ty fit-ty and a ma-ma fit-ty, foo.

2. "Stop," said the ma-ma fish-ie, "or you will get lost." The three lit-tle fish-ies did-n't wan-na be bossed. The
   "Top," ted de ma-ma fit-ty, "Or oo ill det ost." De fee it-ty fit-ty din-na an-na be bossed. De

3.,4. (See additional lyrics)

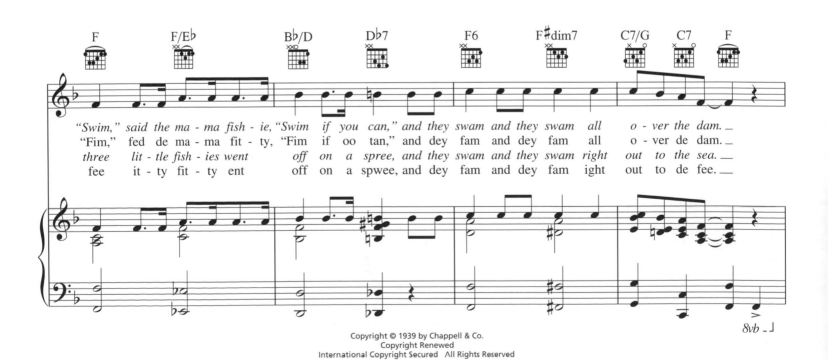

"Swim," said the ma-ma fish-ie, "Swim if you can," and they swam and they swam all o-ver the dam. __
"Fim," fed de ma-ma fit-ty, "Fim if oo tan," and dey fam and dey fam all o-ver de dam. __
three lit-tle fish-ies went off on a spree, and they swam and they swam right out to the sea. __
fee it-ty fit-ty ent off on a spwee, and dey fam and dey fam ight out to de fee. __

8vb

Additional Lyrics

3. *"Whee!" yelled the little fishies, "Here's a lot of fun.*
   We'll swim in the sea till the day is done."
   They swam and they swam and it was a lark,
   Till all of a sudden they saw a shark!

   "Whee!" 'elled de itty fitties, "Ears a wot of fun.
   Ee'll fim in de fee ill de day is un."
   Dey fam and dey fam and it was a wark,
   Till aw of a tudden dey taw a tark!

   Boop boop dittem dattem whattem. Chu!
   Boop boop dittem dattem whattem. Chu!
   Boop boop dittem dattem whattem. Chu!
   Till aw of a tudden dey taw a tark!

4. *"Help!" cried the little fishies, "Gee! Look at all the whales!"*
   And quick as they could they turned on their tails.
   And back to the pool in the meadow they swam,
   And they swam and they swam back over the dam.

   "He'p!" tied de itty fitties, "Dee! Ook at all de fales!"
   And twit as dey tood dey turned on deir tails.
   And bat to de poo in de meddy dey fam,
   And dey fam and dey fam bat over de dam.

   Boop boop dittem dattem whattem. Chu!
   Boop boop dittem dattem whattem. Chu!
   Boop boop dittem dattem whattem. Chu!
   And dey fam and dey fam bat over de dam.

TOMORROW
from the Musical Production ANNIE

Lyric by MARTIN CHARNIN
Music by CHARLES STROUSE

Moderately slow

clears a - way the cob - webs and the sor - row _____ till there's

none. When I'm stuck ___ with a day that's gray and

lone - ly, I just stick ___ out my chin and grin and

say: _____ Oh! the

TWINKLE, TWINKLE LITTLE STAR

Traditional

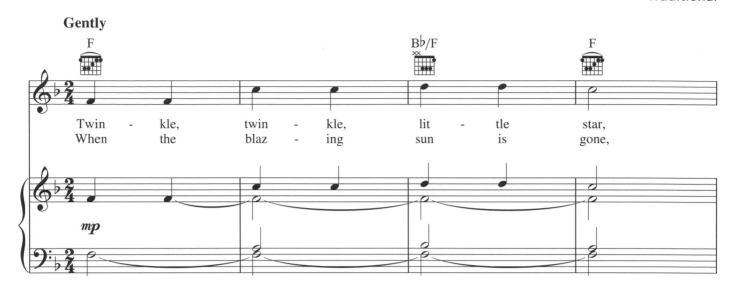

Twin - kle, twin - kle, lit - tle star,
When the blaz - ing sun is gone,

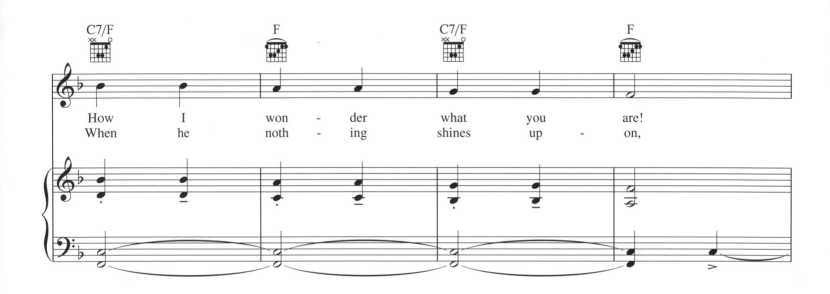

How I won - der what you are!
When he noth - ing what shines up - on,

Up a - bove the world so high,
Then you show your lit - tle light,

Like a dia - mond in the sky.
Twin - kle, twin - kle all the night.

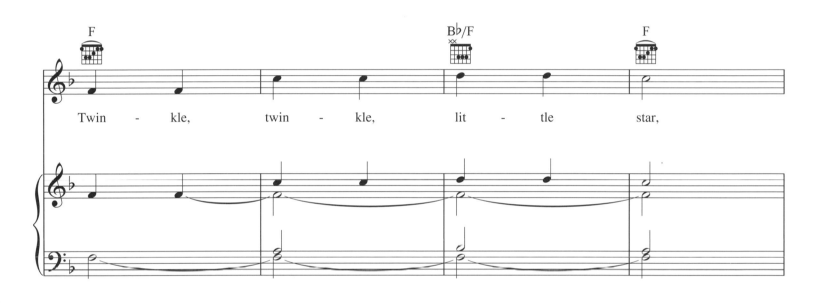

Twin - kle, twin - kle, lit - tle star,

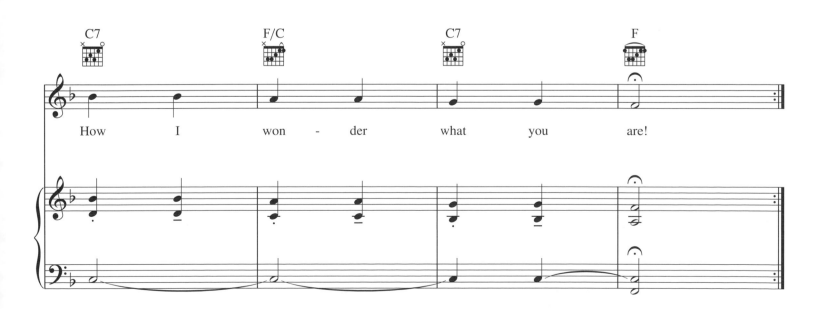

How I won - der what you are!

WHEN I'M SIXTY-FOUR
from YELLOW SUBMARINE

Words and Music by JOHN LENNON
and PAUL McCARTNEY

When I get old - er, los - ing my hair ___ man - y years from now, ___

will you still be send - ing me a val - en - tine, ___

WON'T YOU BE MY NEIGHBOR?
(It's a Beautiful Day in This Neighborhood)
from MISTER ROGERS' NEIGHBORHOOD

Words and Music by
FRED ROGERS

THE WONDERFUL THING
ABOUT TIGGERS

from Walt Disney's THE MANY ADVENTURES OF WINNIE THE POOH

Words and Music by RICHARD M. SHERMAN
and ROBERT B. SHERMAN

Lyrics:

The won-der-ful thing a-bout tig-gers ___ is tig-gers are won-der-ful things! Their tops are made out of rub-ber; ___ their bot-toms are made out of springs! They're bounc-y, trounc-y, flounc-y, pounc-y, Fun! Fun! Fun! Fun!

won-der-ful thing a-bout tig-gers ___ is tig-gers are won-der-ful chaps! They're load-ed with vim and with vig-or; ___ they love to leap in your laps! They're jump-y, bump-y, clump-y, thump-y, Fun! Fun! Fun! Fun!

YELLOW SUBMARINE

from YELLOW SUBMARINE

Words and Music by JOHN LENNON
and PAUL McCARTNEY

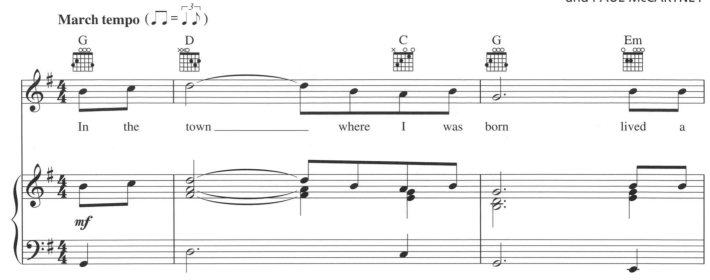

In the town _____ where I was born lived a

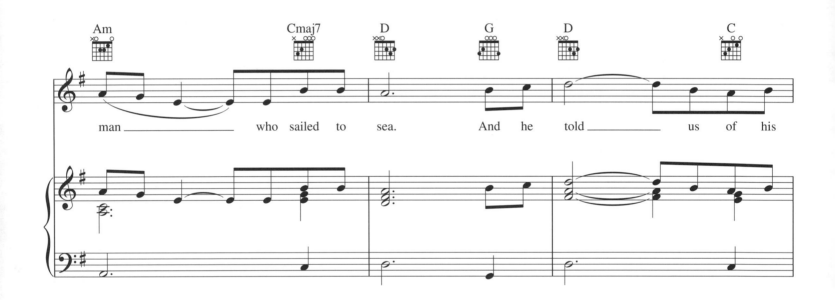

man _____ who sailed to sea. And he told _____ us of his

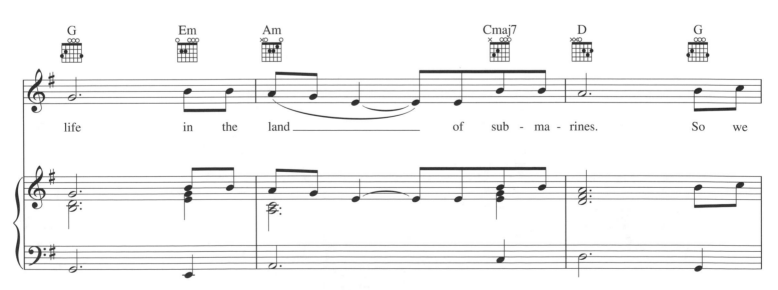

life in the land _____ of sub-ma-rines. So we

YOU'VE GOT A FRIEND IN ME

from Walt Disney's TOY STORY

Music and Lyrics by
RANDY NEWMAN

YANKEE DOODLE

Traditional

Oh, Yan - kee Doo - dle went to town, up -
Fa - ther and I went down to camp, a -

on a lit - tle po - ny. He
long with lit Cap - tain Good - ing, He and

stuck a fea - ther in his cap and
there we saw the in men and boys as

THE ULTIMATE SERIES

This comprehensive series features jumbo collections of piano/vocal arrangements with guitar chords. Each volume features an outstanding selection of your favorite songs. Collect them all for the ultimate music library!

Blues
90 blues classics, including: Boom Boom • Born Under a Bad Sign • Gee Baby, Ain't I Good to You • I Can't Quit You Baby • Pride and Joy • (They Call It) Stormy Monday • Sweet Home Chicago • Why I Sing the Blues • and more.
00310723 . . . . $19.95

Broadway Gold
100 show tunes: Beauty and the Beast • Do-Re-Mi • I Whistle a Happy Tune • The Lady Is a Tramp • Memory • My Funny Valentine • Oklahoma • Some Enchanted Evening • Summer Nights • Tomorrow • many more.
00361396 . . . . $21.95

Broadway Platinum
100 popular Broadway show tunes, featuring: Consider Yourself • Getting to Know You • Gigi • Do You Hear the People Sing • I'll Be Seeing You • My Favorite Things • People • She Loves Me • Try to Remember • Younger Than Springtime • many more.
00311496 . . . . $22.95

Children's Songbook
66 fun songs for kids: Alphabet Song • Be Our Guest • Bingo • The Brady Bunch • Do-Re-Mi • Hakuna Matata • It's a Small World • Kum Ba Yah • Sesame Street Theme • Tomorrow • Won't You Be My Neighbor? • and more.
00310690 . . . . $18.95

Christmas – Third Edition
Includes: Carol of the Bells • Deck the Hall • Frosty the Snow Man • Gesu Bambino • Good King Wenceslas • Jingle-Bell Rock • Joy to the World • Nuttin' for Christmas • O Holy Night • Rudolph the Red-Nosed Reindeer • Silent Night • What Child Is This? • and more.
00361399 . . . . $19.95

Classic Rock
70 rock classics in one great collection! Includes: Angie • Best of My Love • California Girls • Crazy Little Thing Called Love • Joy to the World • Landslide • Light My Fire • Livin' on a Prayer • (She's) Some Kind of Wonderful • Sultans of Swing • Sweet Emotion • and more.
00310962 . . . . $22.95

Classical Collection
Delightful piano solo arrangements, including: Air on the G String (Bach) • Für Elise (Beethoven) • Seguidilla from *Carmen* (Bizet) • Lullaby (Brahms) • Clair De Lune (Debussy) • The Swan (Saint-Saëns) • Ave Maria (Schubert) • Swan Lake (Tchaikovsky) • dozens more.
00311109 . . . . $17.95

Contemporary Christian
Includes over 40 favorites: Awesome God • Can't Live a Day • El Shaddai • Friends • God Is in Control • His Strength Is Perfect • I Can Only Imagine • One of These Days • Place in This World • and more.
00311224 . . . . $19.95

Country – Second Edition
90 of your favorite country hits: Boot Scootin' Boogie • Chattahoochie • Could I Have This Dance • Crazy • Down at the Twist And Shout • Hey, Good Lookin' • Lucille • When She Cries • and more.
00310036 . . . . $19.95

Gospel
Includes: El Shaddai • His Eye Is on the Sparrow • How Great Thou Art • Just a Closer Walk With Thee • Lead Me, Guide Me • (There'll Be) Peace in the Valley (For Me) • Precious Lord, Take My Hand • Wings of a Dove • and more.
00241009 . . . . $19.95

Jazz Standards
Over 100 great jazz favorites: Ain't Misbehavin' • All of Me • Come Rain or Come Shine • Here's That Rainy Day • I'll Take Romance • Imagination • Li'l Darlin' • Manhattan • Moonglow • Moonlight in Vermont • A Night in Tunisia • The Party's Over • Solitude • Star Dust • and more.
00361407 . . . . $19.95

Latin Songs
80 hot Latin favorites, including: Amapola (Pretty Little Poppy) • Amor • Bésame Mucho (Kiss Me Much) • Blame It on the Bossa Nova • Feelings (¿Dime?) • Malagueña • Mambo No. 5 • Perfidia • Slightly out of Tune (Desafinado) • What a Diff'rence a Day Made • and more.
00310689 . . . . $19.95

Love and Wedding Songbook
90 songs of devotion including: The Anniversary Waltz • Canon in D • Endless Love • Forever and Ever, Amen • Just the Way You Are • Love Me Tender • Sunrise, Sunset • Through the Years • Trumpet Voluntary • and more.
00361445 . . . . $19.95

Movie Music – Second Edition
73 favorites from the big screen, including: Can You Feel the Love Tonight • Chariots of Fire • Cruella De Vil • Driving Miss Daisy • Easter Parade • Forrest Gump • Moon River • That Thing You Do! • Viva Las Vegas • The Way We Were • When I Fall in Love • and more.
00310240 . . . . $19.95

New Age
Includes: Cast Your Fate to the Wind • Chariots of Fire • Cristofori's Dream • A Day Without Rain • The Memory of Trees • The Steamroller • and more.
00311160 . . . . $17.95

Nostalgia Songs
100 great favorites from yesteryear, such as: Ain't We Got Fun? • Alexander's Ragtime Band • Casey Jones • Chicago • Danny Boy • Second Hand Rose • Swanee • Toot, Toot, Tootsie! • 'Way Down Yonder in New Orleans • The Yellow Rose of Texas • You Made Me Love You • and more.
00310730 . . . . $17.95

Pop/Rock
70 of the most popular pop/rock hits of our time, including: Bad, Bad Leroy Brown • Bohemian Rhapsody • Dust in the Wind • Imagine • Invisible Touch • More Than Words • Smooth • Tears in Heaven • Thriller • Walking in Memphis • You Are So Beautiful • and more.
00310963 . . . . $22.95

Reggae
42 favorite reggae hits, including: Get Up Stand Up • I Need a Roof • Jamaica Nice • Legalize It • Miss Jamaica • Rivers of Babylon • Tomorrow People • Uptown Top Ranking • Train to Skaville • Try Jah Love • and more.
00311029 . . . . $18.95

Rock 'N' Roll
100 classics, including: All Shook Up • Bye Bye Love • Duke of Earl • Gloria • Hello Mary Lou • It's My Party • Johnny B. Goode • The Loco-Motion • Lollipop • Surfin' U.S.A. • The Twist • Wooly Bully • Yakety Yak • and more.
00361411 . . . . $21.95

Singalong!
100 of the best-loved popular songs ever: Beer Barrel Polka • Crying in the Chapel • Edelweiss • Feelings • Five Foot Two, Eyes of Blue • For Me and My Gal • Indiana • It's a Small World • Que Sera, Sera • This Land Is Your Land • When Irish Eyes Are Smiling • and more.
00361418 . . . . $18.95

Standard Ballads
91 mellow masterpieces, including: Angel Eyes • Body and Soul • Darn That Dream • Day By Day • Easy to Love • Mona Lisa • Moon River • My Funny Valentine • Smoke Gets in Your Eyes • When I Fall in Love • and more.
00310246 . . . . $19.99

Swing Standards
87 songs to get you swinging, including: Bandstand Boogie • Boogie Woogie Bugle Boy • Heart and Soul • How High the Moon • In the Mood • Moonglow • Satin Doll • Sentimental Journey • Witchcraft • and more.
00310245 . . . . $19.95

TV Themes
More than 90 themes from your favorite TV shows, including: The Addams Family Theme • Cleveland Rocks • Theme from Frasier • Happy Days • Love Boat Theme • Hey, Hey We're the Monkees • Nadia's Theme • Sesame Street Theme • Theme from Star Trek® • and more.
00310841 . . . . $19.95

FOR MORE INFORMATION, SEE YOUR LOCAL MUSIC DEALER, OR WRITE TO:

HAL•LEONARD® CORPORATION

7777 W. BLUEMOUND RD. P.O. BOX 13819 MILWAUKEE, WI 53213

www.halleonard.com

THE ULTIMATE SONGBOOKS

HAL•LEONARD

PIANO PLAY-ALONG

These great songbook/CD packs come with our standard arrangements for piano and voice with guitar chord frames plus a CD.

The CD includes a full performance of each song, as well as a second track without the piano part so you can play "lead" with the band!

1. Movie Music
00311072 P/V/G $14.95

2. Jazz Ballads
00311073 P/V/G $14.95

3. Timeless Pop
00311074 P/V/G $14.95

4. Broadway Classics
00311075 P/V/G $14.95

5. Disney
00311076 P/V/G $14.95

6. Country Standards
00311077 P/V/G $14.95

7. Love Songs
00311078 P/V/G $14.95

8. Classical Themes
00311079 Piano Solo $14.95

9. Children's Songs
0311080 P/V/G $14.95

10. Wedding Classics
00311081 Piano Solo................$14.95

11. Wedding Favorites
00311097 P/V/G $14.95

12. Christmas Favorites
00311137 P/V/G $15.95

13. Yuletide Favorites
00311138 P/V/G $14.95

14. Pop Ballads
00311145 P/V/G $14.95

15. Favorite Standards
00311146 P/V/G $14.95

16. TV Classics
00311147 P/V/G $14.95

17. Movie Favorites
00311148 P/V/G $14.95

18. Jazz Standards
00311149 P/V/G $14.95

19. Contemporary Hits
00311162 P/V/G $14.95

20. R&B Ballads
00311163 P/V/G $14.95

21. Big Band
00311164 P/V/G $14.95

22. Rock Classics
00311165 P/V/G $14.95

23. Worship Classics
00311166 P/V/G $14.95

24. Les Misérables
00311169 P/V/G $14.95

25. The Sound of Music
00311175 P/V/G $15.99

26. Andrew Lloyd Webber Favorites
00311178 P/V/G $14.95

27. Andrew Lloyd Webber Greats
00311179 P/V/G $14.95

28. Lennon & McCartney
00311180 P/V/G $14.95

29. The Beach Boys
00311181 P/V/G $14.95

30. Elton John
00311182 P/V/G $14.95

31. Carpenters
00311183 P/V/G $14.95

32. Bacharach & David
00311218 P/V/G $14.95

33. Peanuts™
00311227 P/V/G $14.95

34. Charlie Brown Christmas
00311228 P/V/G $15.95

35. Elvis Presley Hits
00311230 P/V/G $14.95

36. Elvis Presley Greats
00311231 P/V/G $14.95

37. Contemporary Christian
00311232 P/V/G $14.95

38. Duke Ellington – Standards
00311233 P/V/G $14.95

39. Duke Ellington – Classics
00311234 P/V/G $14.95

40. Showtunes
00311237 P/V/G $14.95

41. Rodgers & Hammerstein
00311238 P/V/G $14.95

42. Irving Berlin
00311239 P/V/G $14.95

43. Jerome Kern
00311240 P/V/G $14.95

44. Frank Sinatra – Popular Hits
00311277 P/V/G $14.95

45. Frank Sinatra – Most Requested Songs
00311278 P/V/G $14.95

46. Wicked
00311317 P/V/G $15.99

47. Rent
00311319 P/V/G $14.95

48. Christmas Carols
00311332 P/V/G $14.95

49. Holiday Hits
00311333 P/V/G $14.95

50. Disney Classics
00311417 P/V/G $14.95

51. High School Musical
00311421 P/V/G $19.95

52. Andrew Lloyd Webber Classics
00311422 P/V/G $14.95

53. Grease
00311450 P/V/G $14.95

54. Broadway Favorites
00311451 P/V/G $14.95

55. The 1940s
00311453 P/V/G $14.95

56. The 1950s
00311459 P/V/G $14.95

57. The 1960s
00311460 P/V/G $14.99

58. The 1970s
00311461 P/V/G $14.99

61. Billy Joel Favorites
00311464 P/V/G $14.95

62. Billy Joel Hits
00311465 P/V/G $14.95

63. High School Musical 2
00311470 P/V/G $19.95

64. God Bless America
00311489 P/V/G $14.95

65. Casting Crowns
00311494 P/V/G $14.95

66. Hannah Montana
00311772 P/V/G $19.95

67. Broadway Gems
00311803 P/V/G $14.99

68. Lennon & McCartney Favorites
00311804 P/V/G $14.95

69. Pirates of the Caribbean
00311807 P/V/G $14.95

70. "Tomorrow," "Put on a Happy Face," And Other Charles Strouse Hits
00311821 P/V/G $14.99

71. Rock Band
00311822 P/V/G $14.99

72. High School Musical 3
00311826 P/V/G $19.99

73. Mamma Mia! – The Movie
00311831 P/V/G $14.99

74. Cole Porter
00311844 P/V/G $14.99

FOR MORE INFORMATION, SEE YOUR LOCAL MUSIC DEALER, OR WRITE TO:

HAL•LEONARD®
CORPORATION
7777 W. BLUEMOUND RD. P.O. BOX 13819 MILWAUKEE, WI 53213

Visit Hal Leonard Online at www.halleonard.com

0509